Get your free coloring pages!

Here's how:
1. Visit adultcolouring.com
(UK spelling)
2. Click free pages

If you have any questions or feedback you can contact us at:

Contact@adultcolouring.com

Don't forget to follow us on social media and show us your finished pages!
Links are on our website

www.ingramcontent.com/pod-product-compliance
Lightning Source LLC
LaVergne TN
LVHW081443231224
799792LV00008B/580